The Way IT Is

Also by Chuck Hillig

Enlightenment for Beginners

Looking for God

Seeds for the Soul

The Magic King

The Way IT Is

Realizing the Truth About Everything

Chuck Hillig

SENTIENT PUBLICATIONS

First Sentient Publications edition 2008
Copyright © 2008 by Chuck HIllig

A paperback original

Cover design by Timm Bryson
Book design by Adam Schnitzmeier

Library of Congress Cataloging-in-Publication Data

Hillig, Chuck.
The way it is : realizing the truth about everything / written by Chuck Hillig. -- 2nd ed.
p. cm.
ISBN 978-1-59181-071-1
1. Life. 2. Philosophical anthropology--Miscellanea. 3. Philoso-phy--Miscellanea. I. Title.

BD431.H55 2008
110--dc22
2007043629

Printed in the United States of America
10 9 8 7 6 5 4 3 2 1

SENTIENT PUBLICATIONS
A Limited Liability Company
1113 Spruce Street
Boulder, CO 80302
www.sentientpublications.com

To all of those willing to have the courage to look It straight in the "I" *and laugh!*

Contents

Life — It's a Trip!

Does It really *mean* anything?
Why is It so, well, *strange*?
What's It *really* all about anyway?

Have you ever asked yourself any of these important questions?

Are you still having a hard time trying to figure It all out?

Well, this little book may help you to experience life very differently, and to recognize your life for being what It truly is, deep down!

So, before we start, here's a little hint:

It's not what It's cracked up to be!

Actually, It's *much more*. And *much less!*

So, if you're ready to enlighten up about your life, then here's how to do It.

Okay, So What Is It?

Before we begin, here's a very important question: Are you *sure* that you're really ready to solve the mystery of your life?

Well, if you are, then this book could make it a lot easier for you. It's even possible that you might discover what *everyone's* life is all about.

In fact, after you know Its little secret, you'll probably become more open to just loving It for being what It truly is.

Hey, It's all just too complicated for me. Why do I have to know about Its little secret, anyway? And why do you say that I have to love It?

Well, you should know about It because, as It's often said, "To know It is to love It."

And, learning to love It is actually what It's really all about.

In fact, after you really begin loving It from the bottom of your heart, It could even pop your whole life *insight out!*

So, before we go any further, are you really, *really* sure that you're ready to find out about *It?*

Well, I guess so, but It's just not very clear to me yet. Tell me more about this weird It thing that you keep talking about. I mean, what is It?

Well, first you need to understand that coming up with a universal definition of It has always been a big problem.

It's a big problem? So how is It a problem?

Well, for one thing, nobody can agree on just what to call It! In fact, over the years, It's actually been known by a lot of very different names.

It has different names? Like what?

Well, some people have called It the Tao, or the Holy Spirit, or nirvana, or the Self, or Oneness, or even something called pure Consciousness.

Other cultures have given It very personalized names like Brahman, Shiva, Vishnu, Krishna, Rama, Allah, or Yahweh.

Other folks, however, talk about It as the Universe or maybe they call It the Void. Of course, most Christians in the west usually refer to It as God.

As for me, though, I just like to keep It ordinary, plain and very simple.

Simple? How do you keep It simple?

Easy! I just prefer to call It, well, *It*, and then to let It go at that.

Yes, but calling It It just doesn't seem to be very, well, respectful. Why are you giving It such an ordinary little name?

Well, strange as It sounds, using the word *It* helps me to get down to the bottom line of what It's really all about.

So, how does It do that?

It's because the pronoun *It* cuts straight through a lot of the philosophical gobbledygook that often gets overlaid onto It. Because It makes It all so simple, that's why I call It...*It.*

Yes, but I'm still not getting It! What the hell is this It all about, anyway? I mean, is there any real point to It?

Hey, It's a great question! And, you know, that's what's so incredibly far out about all of It!

What do you mean? What's so far out?

Well, since It's always totally neutral about Itself, there's really no special point to any of It at all!

In fact, I can truthfully say that It is completely *pointless!*

But wait a minute! Why should we even start talking about It if It's all pointless?

Hmm. You're right! It's a very good point!

It seems like you're noticing how easy It is to get confused when we start talking about It.

So, maybe we should just go back to the beginning and take It slowly from the top.

Now, when you say that *It has no point,* or that *It is sunny,* or that *It is amazing,* have you ever stopped to wonder just what this *It* thing is that you're talking about? (Now, relax! It's not a trick question!)

Is that *what It's all about? Look, It can mean anything that I want It to mean. Why are you making such a big deal out of It, anyway? It just doesn't make any sense!*

Actually, you're right about all of It.

For example, It means anything that you want It to mean. It really isn't such a big deal. And It just doesn't make any sense!

Hold It! It's getting much too weird!

Well, just look at how often you say the word *It* in a sentence. Doesn't the word *It* show up all the time in your everyday conversation? I mean, when you get down to It, It's amazingly versatile!

Here, just check It out:

Hey, how's It going?

Let's get It together!

It only hurts for a little while.

Aw, you're so full of It!

They said It couldn't be done.

It put me through a lot of changes.

Let's get It on, homeboy!

Take It or leave It.

Do It to me, baby!

What time is It?

I just can't take It anymore!

It speaks for Itself.

Yes, but what's in It for me?

They just don't get It.

Easy does It.

It really can't be helped.

I've had It up to here!

Let It be.

and on and on and on.

So, here's the Big Question once again: *What is this all inclusive It that we keep talking about?* Actually, a much better question might be, "*What* isn't *It?*"

Look, I don't know what to say about any of It. It's just too much work to figure It all out. Give me another hint about It.

Yes, It *is* hard to put your finger on It.

Okay, well then, here's the so-called long answer: *It just is what It is.*

And if that's still too complicated, then here's the much shorter answer: It just *is*.

Period. The end. Case closed.

Okay, do you have any questions about It?

Hold It! I'm still not getting this whole It thing. I mean, It's just too strange. Give It to me straight. What's this weird It stuff really all about, anyway?

Well, I guess you could say that It's really all about you, and at the very same time, It's also all about me!

Wait! You mean It's about both of us?

Yes, but there's actually much *more* to It than that.

You see, It's also all about *everything*,
And It's all about *everywhere!*

In other words, *It* is all about *what is!*

Yes, but What's
Its Purpose?

So, now are you finally ready to figure out where this It is really coming from, or even where It's going to?

Or maybe you want to discover some ways to have more fun with what It's been doing in your life?

Stop It! It's giving me a headache! I'm still trying to figure out what you're really up to with all of this crazy talk about It.

Well, truthfully, I'm not really up to anything at all!

On the other hand, and at the very same time, It is really up to *absolutely everything!*

For example:

It is up to snuff.

It is up to code.

It is up to the boss.

It is up to speed.

It is up to the traffic.

It is up to the weather.

It is up to no good.

It is up to the courts.

It is up to me

And It is up to you.

Then again, and at the very same time, you can also say that:

It is down the road.

It is down and dirty.

It is downtown.

It is down on Its luck.

It is down in the basement.

It is down and funky.

It is down in the boondocks.

It is downstream.

It is down at the bottom.

It is down at the corner.

It is down in the polls.

You see, because It's up and down and all around, this It that we're talking about doesn't really have any specific location.

And, without having a location, It can't ever take a point of view about anything!

So, since It doesn't have any special viewpoint about things, It's absolutely impossible for you to guess just what It'll be doing next!

Well, just because It doesn't have a specific viewpoint, why would that still make this It thing so unpredictable?

Well, It's unpredictable because, at any given moment, It's able to be on *opposite* sides of the same thing at the very same time. Here, check out these flip-flops:

It was so funny!

No, It was absolutely terrible.

You have to take care of It.

No, you'd better just leave It alone.

It really is a crying shame!

No, It's really a very lucky break.

It's half empty.

No, It's actually half full.

It was the best of times.

No, It was the worst of times.

etc., etc., etc.

Back and forth, back and forth.

You see, It can be used to describe *all* of the parts of the very same experience, at the very same moment!

But if It has so many different meanings at the same time, how will I ever be able to know just what, or even where, this It really is?

Ah, but you see, that's exactly my point. The truth of It is, you won't know!

One minute, you'll think that you see It, but then the very next moment, you'll think that you don't see It.

That's because Its mysterious nature is to be on both sides of the very same coin (and, to be the whole coin too)...at the very same time!

You see, It's really very clever!

Well, It may be clever, but It's also pretty strange, too. Okay, so what does this It want from me, anyway?

Oh, It wants nothing. Nada! Zip! Zero!

In truth, It neither wants nor expects anything from you at all.

Not now. Not ever!

And, besides, there's really *nothing* that you could ever give It that would make any kind of difference to It whatsoever.

Well, now I am getting a bit more curious about It. So, what can I do with this It thing, anyway?

Well, you can't really improve upon It in any way at all. In fact, you're completely and totally stuck with It *being exactly the way It is.*

So, even though it might make you a bit uneasy to think about It, there's absolutely *nothing* at all that you can ever do about It, or to It, or even for It.

But the really ironic part of It all is that *you can't make a single solitary move on your own without It!*

So, when you think about It, maybe It's best to just give It all up and completely surrender to It!

There's simply no way at all that you'll ever be able to change anything about the way It is! Period!

But why can't I just stop doing It?

Well, since you've been doing It for such a long time now, your doing It has become kind of a, well, habit.

In fact, you may be surprised to discover that, at a very deep level, you've even gotten yourself hooked on doing It.

But here's a very strange paradox:

At the very same time, It has also been hooking Itself on doing you!

So now, maybe you're beginning to see that there's really a lot more to It than meets the I.

But Is It
Really Practical?

❋ *Well, if I can't do anything about It, or to It, or for It, can I at least do something with It?*

Yes, you're always free to try to do something with It, but It still won't make any real difference to It at all!

In short, It will simply be the way that It will be.

And, amazingly, It doesn't even know why.

So, since you can't really mix It up or sort It out, maybe It would be best for you to embrace It for being exactly how It is.

Yes, but, why should I embrace any of It at all? I mean, It just doesn't seem like It's really good for anything.

Well, you're absolutely right!

It really isn't good for anything at all.

But, on the other hand, It isn't bad for anything, either.

And, even though It doesn't make any special claims to being right, at the very same time, It's not denying that It's being wrong!

Remember that *It's simply unable to take an exclusive stance about anything at all.*

Not ever! In short, It is always positionless!

I'll say it again: Instead, of being over here or over there, It's always occupying every possible side of every possible issue simultaneously.

When you think about It, isn't It totally amazing?

Even though you're learning more about how It all works, maybe It still seems pretty puzzling to you.

Luckily, you don't have to worry about trying to figure It all out right now because It's always going on in your life all of the time.

In fact, if you're really mixed up about It, then you're undoubtedly right on Its schedule.

You see, It really *wants* you to feel confused and uncertain about Its true nature.

And It's able to hook your interest in It by acting very mysterious.

In other words, as strange as It may seem, It wants to distract you from learning about Its incredible little secret.

Well, It must be working because I'm sure not getting It. Why is It distracting me? And just what is this so-called incredible little secret anyway?

Well, the secret is that, underneath it all, It's just been playing this big, fantastic game with (drum roll and *Ta Da!)*

Itself!

And, in order to keep Its game going, It always tries to keep you diverted so that you won't go blowing the whistle on Its fun. Well, at least, not too soon.

So, here's my best advice: Just relax!

It's only trying to have a good time playing out Its little game. So you don't need to take all of the crazy soap opera melodrama that It creates for Itself in your life so darned, well, personally.

But if It's only playing out a silly little game with Itself, then exactly who is It that It's playing with, anyway?

Well, that's just what's so damn funny about all of It because It's a big surprise!

Since It is really the only one here, then, obviously, It can only be playing both with, and as, you!

You see, in order to play out Its little game, It has to first use you in order for you to use It.

The little ego-self that you think you are has actually been a kind of gift that It's been giving to Itself in order to play out Its game.

But, in this special case, *the gift and the gift giver are the same!*

In other words, although there's only one player (It) who's, seemingly, doing It all, the game becomes a lot more fun when It pretends that there's a lot more stuff going on.

Why would It do that? It sure seems to be a pretty strange little game.

No, not really. For example, do you remember way back when you were a kid, and you liked to play tag with the other kids?

Well, you'd all pretend that the one who was tagged was called It.

Yeah. So?

So, just like then, It is playing a cosmic game of tag. With you!

Or, to put It another way, you have been officially designated as *It!*

The only difference is that, right now, you are pretending not to know It!

Okay, How Does It Play Its Little Game?

If there's really nothing else but It, how is It even possible for It to be able to play out this crazy game just by Itself?

Well, It's really simple! I mean, when you think about It, the answer is pretty obvious.

You see, in order for It to be able to pull It off, It first has to pretend, very very hard, that It's not really It.

Why would that be so important?

Once It *pretends* that It's not *really* It, then It can start pretending that It needs to go out into the world to start looking for Itself!

Now, remember, the key idea here is that, although It *looks* for Itself, It doesn't actually *find* Itself.

You see, the real drama and excitement of the game comes when It pretends (often very ingeniously) that It just can't seem to find Itself anywhere at all!

So It looks, and It looks, and It looks, but, (poor baby), It just doesn't seem to be able to find Itself anywhere at all! *(sob, sob!)*

It may sound a bit silly to you, but this is actually how It plays out Its game!

But, wait a minute! It's totally crazy! I mean, doesn't It ever get to find Itself?

Yes, of course It does!

The irony is that It actually ends up finding Itself absolutely everywhere!

Since It's the only player in the game, It's just going to be *meeting Itself, again and again, over and over.*

(I mean, who else is there besides It?)

In short, wherever It goes to look for Itself, there It already is, looking back!

But, here's how It gets really tricky: in order to keep the game going, It has to keep pretending very hard that It's just not able to recognize Itself, *as Itself!*

You see, by hiding Itself behind a lot of very clever disguises, It can better pretend that It's just forgotten who It *really* is and what It *really* looks like.

And just let me tell you what happens when It starts to fool Itself like that!

It starts creating a lot of drama for Itself by taking on some very righteous beliefs like:

No! You're wrong! That's not It!

Or maybe It'll say something like:

"Oh I know where It's at. It's over on that mountain with that enlightened guru!"

Or even:

"It just depends on your karma!"

Or maybe It'll start to argue:

"No, the answers to what It's all about are written down right here in these very holy books!"

And, all too often, It likes to take on Its favorite disguise by stating dogmatically:

"My spiritual path is the real Truth about It all! It's the only way that you can get to Heaven!"

So, are you starting to get It yet?

It's all a great big put-on!

Can you begin to appreciate now just how cleverly It's been hiding from Itself?

You see, as long as It's pretending to go out into the world *looking for Itself*, then It can also continue to pretend that It's not really *being Itself* (well, at least for a while.)

You know, when you think about all of the melodramatic changes that It puts Itself through in trying to rediscover Itself, It really is incredibly funny!

But why do you think that It's so damn funny? I have a lot of big problems!

Well, It's funny because, deep down, It creates *all* of Its big problems for Itself.

But, at the very same time, It's also creating all of Its own solutions, too!

The greatest irony is that It pretends to be all of the opposing sides of the problems that show up in the game. Yes! All of them!

But underneath It all, It's still going to turn out okay because It knows very well what It's doing. After all, It's used to playing Its game.

The great fun of It, though, is pretending that It just doesn't quite remember It all.

As you've already noticed by now, It's very, very good at completely fooling Itself whenever It's really into playing this far out game of make believe!

Still, every once in a while, It often likes to give Itself a little change of pace.

Change of pace? What do you mean?

At certain times in your life, you'll seem to experience It more intimately.

Then, after a while, maybe you just won't be able to feel It around you quite as much as you did before.

But It's all Okay. Just relax and take It all in.

Since It's always happening to you, you don't need to worry about any of Its so-called changes.

You see, sometimes, It will *seem* to come a little bit closer to you, but then, after a while, It will *seem* to go away from you again.

One minute, you may think, *Yes, I really do get It,* but, then, later on, you'll start to think, *Oh no! I just don't get It anymore.*

Even though It's not really going anywhere, It will often make you go through cycles of Now-you're-getting-It and, later on, Now-you're-*not*-getting-It, again and again. Who knows why? It's inscrutable!

Best advice: As It's showing up for you, don't cling to any of It at all. Just lighten up and let It do Its thing. It's really all okay!

And here's the *best* news about It: You don't have to be afraid of losing It because none of It can ever really *die.*

Not ever!

Why? Simply because It was never *born* to begin with!

Remember, It just is!

And It's always been happening right there in front of you, 100 percent of the time.

Nothing about It is ever missing or incomplete. In fact, It is Its very nature to be fully present for you in Its absolute totality, every single second!

Maybe It's here right now, but how do I know that It'll always be fully present for me wherever I happen to go? I mean, will It always be with me?

Well, of *course* It will!

There's just no place else for It to ever *be!*

In other words, this, *right here and right now, is always* where *It's at.*

So How Can
I See It?

❋ *If It's always been that near to me, why don't I recognize It up close? I mean, what does It usually look like?*

Well, It has countless ways to appear:

angry, boring, childish, depressed, edgy, foolish, grim, happy, ignorant, jolly, kind, loving, moody, nasty, obsessed, paranoid, quick, resistant, spooky, teasing, unsure, violent, wistful, x-rated, yucky, and zany.

Because It has an infinite number of faces, you'll just never be able to predict exactly *how* It will be appearing for you next!

Now are you finally beginning to see just how cleverly It's been playing this little game with you?

Yes, I think I'm getting It.

Well, then you'd better hang onto your precious little ego, because It's about to get even wilder!

Okay. If you're ready, then here It comes:

You've never known what was coming down the road next for *one big simple reason:*

It is the only one who's actually been in the so-called driver's seat of your entire life, from the first day that you were, supposedly, born!

In other words, It has been calling *all* of the shots for you and making *all* of your decisions!

That's right! Absolutely *all* of them!

Yes, yes I know what you're going to say.

All this time, you've believed that wonderful little *you*, in all of your "infinite" wisdom, were in charge of at least *some* of what was going on!

Well, here It comes! Surprise, surprise!

You see, that's been one of the cleverest parts of this whole game!

The *you* that you *think* you are has really *never* been in charge *of anything at all!*

Not now! Now ever!

In short, It has really been taking you.

It's been taking me? Taking me where?

It's been taking you for the ride of your life!

But, how has It been doing that? Hey, what's really going on here, anyway?!

Well, first of all, It's really the One that's been making you *seem* to think things and *seem* to feel things.

What?!

And, on top of that, It's also the One that's been making you seem to say things and seem to do things!

In fact, sooner or later, you'll just have to accept It all!

Accept It all? Well, exactly what is It that I'm going to have to accept?

Eventually, you'll just have to accept It for being the incredible paradox that It actually is.

Oh, really? So what's this big paradox that I have to accept?

Well, even though you're totally responsible for It, this very same It has still been controlling every single aspect of your life!

Yes! That's right! Every single aspect!

You see, at the bottom line, you have only been thinking *Its* thoughts.

You have only been feeling *Its* feelings.

You have only been speaking *Its* words.

You have only been doing *Its* actions.

In short, the *you* that you *think* you are hasn't been doing *any* of It.

Wait! Then who's been doing it?

Well, in truth, the *It-That-Is* has really been doing *you!*

Doing me! Hey, I just don't like the sound of that at all. How can It be doing me?! I mean, It just doesn't seem to be fair!

Hey, It's not a big deal. It doesn't have to be fair. And It's certainly okay if you don't like how It is. You see, It really doesn't matter either way.

It's all so totally crazy! How is It even possible? You're saying that I'm not in charge of my own life! It's nuts!

Yep! It has been in charge of absolutely *everything* in your entire life from the very first day. *No exceptions!*

But doesn't any of It really matter?

Well yes, of course It matters!

If *you* say It matters.

But isn't any of It important?

Of course It's important!

If *you* say It's important.

Yes, but doesn't any of It mean anything?

Yes, of course It means something!

If *you* say It means something.

You see, It only wants what *you* want. It only fears what *you* fear.

In short, *It all depends entirely on you!*

But what would It do if It had to deal with all of my everyday problems? Why won't It do something to help me?

Well, just look at what It has been doing in your life. I mean, after all, you're the one standing there in Its shoes!

Listen, don't get so worked up about It because It really *does* give you a lot of big breaks.

Big breaks? Yeah, right! Well what kind of big breaks has It given me?

Well, for example, It's never judged you as being wrong or bad.

Okay, so It hasn't judged me. So what?

Well, that means there's nothing for It to ever forgive you for! It's all really okay!

And It's also not been picking on you or punishing you or trying to get Its revenge.

But, here is Its *biggest* break:

It doesn't even need to *save* you from anything because there's nothing really out there for It to be saving you from!

This, just as It is, is really It!

The great mystery in all of this is that It finds Its true source in the deepest center of *your* heart of hearts.

And that's exactly why It will always be taking very special care of you.

In fact, It dearly loves you *just as much as It loves Itself.*

And, as your beloved, It's even *closer* to you than your very own breath!

Now do you have a better idea about how It's all put together?

You see, you are *exactly* what It's been looking for! And, of course, *vice versa.*

You are not a part of It, *and* you are not apart from It.

Why? Because It simply can't have any parts. It can only *pretend* to have parts.

And *who-you-think-you-are* is the name of the number one part that It's pretending to have.

Then Its other pretend parts start playing out a fascinating drama with the *who-you-think-you-are* as the number one Star! So, start starring!

This cosmic (comic?) drama has a lot of movable sets and props, helpful allies, brave heroes and heroines, evil villains, temporary walk-ons, and is currently supported by *a cast of over 6.5 billion extras! Wow!*

And, since It's acting like a kind of movie screen to Itself, It's very happy to support all of the many different parts that It's pretending are being projected onto It. So, here's the bottom line:

It's all only a great big story!

This melodramatic movie that you're starring in (better known as *your life)* is only an entrancing tale that It's been telling *to Itself!*

Your cosmic costume is the mask of your ego that It's only been projecting onto Itself.

So when you become aware enough to start keeping an *I* out for your own inner reflection, you'll begin to see *It* absolutely *everywhere.*

For example, It's *in your face,* and It's also *behind your back.*

It's *over your head,* but It's also *under your feet.*

It's in your ears, in your mouth, and It's even *flowing in your veins.*

You're eating It,
Drinking It,
Touching It,
Smelling It,
and even sitting on It!

It's the cosmic fingertip that's only able to point to Itself!

No, you really can't deny It any longer, so here It comes:

Yes! It's true! You really are It!

Isn't It absolutely amazing how One-derfully It all turns out in the end?!

Yes, but if It is really true, then how can I best learn to live with It?

You can start doing It today by fully embracing your life both *with*, and *as*, the *It-That-You-Are*.

Participate in It with complete awareness by fully celebrating the incredible things around you that, each and every moment, are unfolding just for *you!*

After all, It doesn't want you to be an unappreciative audience to your very own melodrama! So, start enjoying the chaos!

Since It's all an incredible gift, you could even start frolicking with all of It as Its very willing dance partner.

In fact, you actually love It more when you allow yourself to begin playing with It joyfully.

Playing with It? But, why would I ever want to play with It?

Well, why *not* play with It? Look, just turn It around. I mean, isn't It having a lot of fun playing with *you?*

Yeah, well I guess It's having fun.

Okay, then don't put It off any longer. Just go ahead and throw yourself into It by loving It *totally,* right here *and* right now, *being exactly the way that It is.*

Learn to trust It completely by freely and consciously *choosing whatever It is* that It's choosing for *you.*

Honor and respect It for being *the way It is and* for being *the way It isn't!*

When you're loving It enough to fully dance Its cosmic dance, then you are truly *being* the It-That-You-Are.

Remember, the life that you're living, no matter what may be unfolding for you, is the perfect expression of the incredible love affair that It's having with Itself, right here and right now.

So embrace It lovingly in your heart for being the very special blessing that It truly is.

When you do, you'll discover that Its source is the very purest expression of a profound and infinite love. *And It's a love that you already are!*

Okay, Then Show It to Me!

So, now are you ready to see what It *really* looks like when It's *not* wearing one of Its usual disguises?

Well, turn the page and you'll see one of my favorite pictures of It.

To *really* get It, please use scissors to cut It out!

So, here It is!
It sure *looks* like It, doesn't It?

And *this* is what It looks like from behind!

Please cut It out with scissors from the *other* side of this page.

Now, hold It close to you and try looking through It. Move It around and really notice how It's showing up for you.

Try holding your thumb on one side of It, and your forefinger on the other side.

If you press them together slowly, *you can actually touch It!*

Twenty Questions

❋ For those who feel the need to get really serious about It.

POINT OF DEPARTURE: When Consciousness *pretends* that there's a separation between what It says It *is* (the I), and what It says It *isn't* (the not-I), then the world mysteriously reappears. But It's not really going anywhere. Remember that the purpose of a song is not to arrive at the final note. The purpose of a song is found in the joyous singing of It. So it is with Consciousness. In other words, It's just singing!

Q: But Chuck, It really can't be that basic. Aren't you simplifying this whole thing a little bit too much?

A: How can you oversimplify something that is, by Its very nature, simplicity Itself? In fact, because Its simplicity is absolutely complete and pure, It can only manifest Itself by *pretending* to be complex. In other words, when the indivisible Consciousness pretends to be divided into parts, It creates an illusory world of polarities. And you already are that very Consciousness, Itself!

Q: *Yes, but if I'm really this so-called It, then why don't I have a direct and personal experience of being It right now?*

A: This "you," (the illusory ego-self that you *think* you are), can never personally experience Its own true, fundamental nature. You can only be what It *already is* (i.e., It). In other words, you will never be able to get It simply because It already *is* It! Or, to put It another way, how can you ever arrive at a place where you are already dwelling?

Believing that you're not really there, however, provides the cosmic momentum for It to, seemingly, go out looking for Itself.

It's this purposeful misidentification that sets the entire drama of your life into (e)motion.

Q: Well, if any of It is really true, how can I actually use this philosophy in my everyday life?

A: You can't use It in the usual sense because, actually, It will only be using you. At one level, though, you can stay more aligned with It by consciously choosing exactly what It appears to be choosing for you.

In other words, practice saying a resounding *Yes!* to whatever shows up for you. And, even when you feel like saying *no*, then just say *yes* to the fact that, *at least for that moment*, you're saying *no*.

It's best, though, to always make *Yes!* your default position in life. Don't reject anything, *not even your own rejections!*

Remember, however, that *you*, (the historical ego-self) are only pretending that you're able to manipulate or control It. Consciousness will always get Its own way in the end, simply because, no matter where you think your ego-self is going, It is already there, waiting for you.

Q: Is this why you say that It is always directly in front of me in Its absolute totality?

A: Yes. I mean, where else could It possibly be? By definition, there can't be some of It here and then some more of It around the corner, too. That would be implying that It could, somehow, be divided from Itself. But, if It's absolutely simple and complete, then *It can't really have any parts at all.* It can only pretend to have parts. The you that you think you are is only one of the many parts that It is pretending to have.

So whatever is in your experience at this very instant is absolutely *all of It.* There's really nothing and nowhere else. Or, to put it another way, through Its own I's (*your* I's), It sees 100 percent of Itself, 100 percent of the time. None of It is ever missing simply because none of It can ever be left out.

Not ever!

It's right there in front of you, in Its absolute totality, *all of the time.*

Q: But where does our idea of God come in?

A: As I said earlier, God really doesn't come into It at all. God actually comes *out of It*. The word *God* (or *the Self, Allah, Yahweh, Spirit,* etc.) is simply the ego's attempt to give a more formal name to the unnamable *It-That-Is*.

It's like a movie actor who's trying to name the underlying screen that he believes is necessary for his unfolding drama to be made manifest.

The greatest obstacle, though, is the actor's ego based wish to be a personal witness to his own awakening to this truth.

However, that's completely impossible. Why? There can't be a separate person present at the so-called awakening, because there isn't a separate person present right now, who's not awakened.

In other words, there's *nothing* for this actor to get. There isn't a separate actor present who's available to be getting It or, *not* getting It in the first place! In short, all that there truly *is*, is the seamless and unbroken Screen of Pure Consciousness, Itself, this mysterious It. After all, It is all *One*.

Q: Yes, but what does that do to this whole idea of choice? I mean, doesn't free will really exist?

A: Before addressing that question, you need to determine if there are separate individuals out there who are truly present and real.

You see, if *all* separation is an illusion, then any discussion about some illusory self having a free will or not would be as useless as arguing about the probable water temperature of a lake mirage out in the desert.

Just like there's no real lake out there with a water temperature, there's also no real separate self present which could have (or not have) a so-called free will.

Q: But what does that notion do to the idea of karma, reincarnation and the law of cause and effect? Are any of those ideas real?

A: Well, yes and no. At one level, karma and reincarnation *do* exist, but neither of them is actually *real*. These two phenomena persist as long as there continues to be the illusion of a separate and an individual self who believes that he is the so-called do-er.

Here's how It seems to work: If you consider yourself to be setting up causes, either good or bad, you're automatically implying that, sooner or later, you'll have to be experiencing their effects either good or bad. Cause and effect always arise simultaneously.

But, if all separation is illusory, then exactly *who* is actually experiencing the phenomena of cause and effect?

In other words, who, specifically, is all of this life and death drama involving karma and reincarnation happening to? *Who's the "who?"*

If all there is, is Consciousness, then exactly *who is being reincarnated here?*

Or, for that matter, *who* really died in the first place in order to be reborn?

Q: So are you saying that all of mankind's past history is only part of this great illusion, and that none of it ever really happened!?

A: There's only One so-called movie playing on the Cosmic Screen, and It's always the very drama that's surrounding *you.*

So, did mankind's history ever really happen? Consider this: When you watch a movie, did the off-screen events that are referred to by the characters in the film really take place at all? No, of course not. But the dramatic story on the screen is greatly advanced (and enhanced) by the viewer's willingness to pretend that those off-screen events being referred to did, in fact, actually occur.

But It (the Cosmic Movie) is always fully present in Its *absolute totality*, right there in front of you. Nothing is ever being left out.

In short, this really is It, and It's all happening just for you in this very precious moment of Now.

Q: Yes, but what about the future? It almost sounds like you're saying that I shouldn't try to do anything about it.

A: No, I'm not suggesting that at all. For example, if It moves you to save the whales, help the poor, stop the spread of HIV, etc., then go ahead and throw yourself into It 100 percent. Don't hold anything back! Go ahead and do It.

The you that you think you are, though, is not really the do-er or the true source of any of these actions. Consequently, this same you need not concern Itself with the results of any of these actions that It's feeling compelled to do.

Remember that Consciousness is only sourcing Itself. So, by playing out *all* of the so-called parts, Consciousness is the only One that's really *doing* any of It. It's the only game in town!

In truth, there's nothing else (and no one else) present at all. *You* are not really here. Only *It* is here. And, although It uses different mouths, It's only been having a *monologue*.

As strange as It sounds, It is totally alone!

Or, to put It another way, *It is All One.*

Q: But are you saying that I shouldn't really care about how things work out?

A: Actually, I'm just suggesting that you play out your role in the cosmic drama with gusto and passion. Remember, though, that you can remain truly detached from what shows up for you only if you give up your idea about what working out looks like. In truth, *things will neither work out nor will they not work out*. They will only be whatever they will be.

If you overlay what you think *should* be happening on top of what actually *is* happening, that's only a manifestation of the ego-self pretending to be the do-er of what's unfolding. *But, in truth, It is doing It all.*

The irony here is that, even though it doesn't really matter what you do in your role, It's still very important that you go ahead and do It anyway.

After all, the dance is best honored when the dancer (It) dances the dance, *even if It means that, sometimes, It's going to be stepping on Its very own toes!*

It's all only a dazzling display of colors in a cosmic kaleidoscope. The nature of the Consciousness that you are is to *be* what It is, by pretending to, seemingly, become what It's pretending to not be.

Q: Are you enlightened?

A: Well, if all divisions on the Cosmic Screen are illusory, then how is individual enlightenment even possible?

In other words, what separate being is ever really there to be enlightened (or, for that matter, to be unenlightened) in the first place?

Q: But isn't any of It real?

A: No matter what activities are happening in the movie, the fundamental reality beneath It all is still only the unbroken and seamless screen that's supporting *all* of the dramas that are being played out upon It.

Although the world appears to exist, *the only thing that's really real is Consciousness Itself.*

So, as the historical ego-self that you think you are, you've always been looking directly into the cosmic mirror of life Itself, and beholding the wondrous and multifaceted face of God.

The incredible miracle is that It's always been *your* face!

Q: *So, then, why is everyone seeking some sort of enlightenment, this It?*

A: In truth, you already *are* who you are looking for. Enlightenment is *not* the attainment of anything new. Instead, It is more like a discovery of the essential truth about what actually *is*. Your personal drama, though, will continue to magically unfold around you exactly as It does. You won't really awaken *from* the dream as much as you'll awaken *to* the dream.

But, in this awakening, the Dreamer has to disappear entirely. If not, he'll just substitute one dream called *once I was asleep* for a newer dream that's called *now I am awake!* And here's the great cosmic irony: The self who is asleep is also the very same self who is awake. After all, there's only *one* self. Only *one* Consciousness. Only *one* It.

The mesmerizing seductiveness of the dream is seen in the longstanding belief that, someday, if the Dreamer only plays his cosmic cards right, he will eventually awaken. But, in truth, the enlightenment bus that he's been waiting for will never show up for him. Why? Well, by expecting that some *future* awakening may occur for him somewhere in time, he's only reinforcing his belief that the very same Consciousness he is seeking is not 100 percent fully *present* for him, right here and right now. *But It always is.*

Q: Isn't there some kind of objective reality in the world? What about the idea of good and evil? Don't they really exist, even as a small part of this universal Consciousness?

A: It might help you to consider that Consciousness (It) is a kind of context or space that *appears* to contain a world of polarities. But, at the very heart of truth, there's really no success or failure. There's no right and no wrong; no good and no bad; no victors and no victims; no heaven and no hell and no life and no death.

All of these polarities only appear on the subjective spectrum of opposites that It creates for Itself in order to play out Its cosmic drama.

In a sense, these opposites appear to radiate out in all directions from the point of view that you (as your historical ego-self) *think* that you have. It, however, contains It all.

Q: What can I do to improve myself spiritually? Don't I need to change in some way?

A: But how can *who* you are really change? Your basic nature is *pure Consciousness.* Essentially, you are infinite, omnipresent, impersonal, omniscient, and immutable. As such, there is nothing that you need to remember, to learn about, to realize, to strive for, to pray to or to meditate on.

In fact, It's the very belief that real change and spiritual progress is possible that provides the momentum for you (as the historical ego-self) to want to propel your story forward and out into some kind of illusory future where you can, hopefully, become satisfied, sanctified, or made more whole.

But, in truth, you can't ever become any more of who you *already* are.

Why not?

Because you already *are* whatever It is that you are seeking.

Q: What about all of the current interest in metaphysics? Won't It help me to study things like astrology, ESP, tarot, crystals, channeling and so forth? Why wouldn't my growth in those esoteric areas be a very positive sign of my spiritual progress?

A: Although the study of metaphysics is neither good nor bad, It often proves Itself to be a time consuming diversion for many people. When you're spiritually seduced by the promise that you can attain special knowledge or powers, It's easy for the seeker to become unwittingly distracted from his true inner quest.

Consequently, instead of helping the seeker to look inside to discover the truth about who he really is, these esoteric and pseudo-spiritual practices often only give the seeker something else to get attached to or, even worse, to feel superior about.

Playing the game of spiritual one-upmanship is a subtle ploy that's often used by the ego to avoid the possibility of experiencing personal annihilation in the face of Its own infinite vastness.

Q: So how do you suggest that I learn to live with myself being this infinite Consciousness?

A: Does an ocean wave really need to find the ocean? You already are whatever It is that you're seeking. So, just commit yourself 100 percent to doing whatever It is that you're doing, *but do It consciously and with an open hearted sense of detached compassion and total love.*

Avoid judging or discriminating against anyone in any way. Other people are neither bad nor good. They just are as they are. Period. After all, doesn't an author love his villains every bit as much as he loves his heroes?

Touch life softly, and live each moment as if you're arriving at It, and departing from It, at the very same instant.

Consciousness will appear to tease you, seduce you, scare you, amaze you, and, from time to time, even try to overwhelm and destroy you. Oftentimes after It scares you to death, It thrills you to life. But learn to fully embrace It as *who you are* because It's just doing the incredible dance of the divine. After all, It's the very play of Consciousness, Itself!

And, remember that all of It is being staged for your own delight and edification! Welcome It all joyfully, with a sense of deep gratitude and profound wonder.

Your being able to play in the world is a miraculous gift that Consciousness is giving to Itself, so always be an appreciative audience to your own melodrama. All of It is just for *you*.

Let *everything* happen to you because It's really all okay, right here and right now, *being the way It is!*

Remember, the so-called purpose of any dance is *not* for the dancer's body to end up in some final, frozen position. The real purpose of any dance is only found in the actual dancing of the dance, Itself!

Since you can't get out of It, then just get further into It.

So, whatever happens to show up in your drama, *just keep on dancing, right where you are!*

Q: Won't I need some kind of dance teacher to help me with all of It?

A: Yes. A teacher is necessary, but you need to give up your idea about what this teacher might actually look like. The guru may not show up for you as a physical human being.

However, the guru (It) is ever present, and It's always appearing directly in front of you as everything, and everyone, that you're pretending you're *not*. And, since the experiences that show up for the historical ego-self are, in fact, the guru's deepest teaching, you can't get lost.

You need to trust that this grace will slowly begin to awaken you from your delusion of separation. Whatever's happening in your life at this very moment is the golden path that It has chosen to lead you to your awakening. The drama unfolds when you've forgotten that *you* have chosen It being exactly as It is.

And so here is yet another very strange paradox: *It turns out to be Its own guru!*

Q: Well, does this philosophy have some kind of special name?

A: Yes, It does. This is a taste of the cross-cultural perennial philosophy that has appeared in all societies and cultures. In India, for example, It's known as Advaita, the ancient path of direct insight and knowledge. It's really the *wayless way* because the seeker is not focused primarily on the ritualistic devotion, surrender or outward activity that's usually found on many of the other paths.

The emphasis here is to use the power of self inquiry to seek out the source of the belief in I by asking yourself the ultimate, primordial question: "Who am I?"

As all of the answers to that mind-stopping question slowly drop away, you awaken to find yourself in a place in the heart that you *never really left.*

At that pointless point of awareness, your ground of being becomes, quite simply, *I am,* and you recognize the very essence of who you *really* are: *Love. Loving Itself!*

Q: *Okay, but quite honestly, how can any of this strange stuff help the real world?*

A: Well, is it the so-called real world that's asking this question, or is it only the "you" whom you *think* you are?

Your spiritual work lies in discovering for *whom* this question is arising.

As Ramana Maharshi said, "The answer to life's problems is to first see 'who' has them!"

And so, It is.

What Others Have Said About It

❀ If It were not laughed at, It would not be the Tao.

—*Lao Tzu*

The question is not what should I do in the future to get It, but, rather, what am I presently doing that prevents me from realizing It right now?

—*Alan Watts*

If the doors of perception were cleansed, then everything would appear to man as It is: infinite.

—*William Blake*

Everything is perfect in being what It is. It has nothing to do with good or bad.

—Longchenpa

The Self, though One, takes the shape of every object in which It dwells.

—The Upanishads

Everything that happens, happens as It should.

—Marcus Aurelius

Just allow It.

—Francis Lucille

Never the Spirit is born; never the time when It was not.

—from a Sioux prayer

The game is not about becoming somebody; It is about becoming nobody!

—Ram Dass

It cannot be called the void or the not-void, or both or neither; but in order to point It out, It is called the Void.

—*Nagarjuna*

It is all only a great game of pretending.

—*Ramana Maharshi*

It (life) should be lived as a play.

—*Plato*

It puts obstacles in the way. It weaves a net and then gets entangled in It.

—*Sathya Sai Baba*

It (human life) is an endless illusion.

—*Blaise Pascal*

God has created the world in play. It is God Himself who is sporting in the form of Man.

—*Ramakrishna*

Every man is divinity in disguise. It is God playing the fool.

—*Ralph Waldo Emerson*

It does not matter much what happens.

—*Nisargadatta*

It is always Now.

—*Eckhart Tolle*

It is Eternity Itself. It is here and now.

—*Swami Krishnananda*

For every one that asks, receives; and to him that knocks, It shall be opened.

—*Jesus*

Who can explain It? Who can tell you why? Fools give you reasons; Wise men never try.

—*Some Enchanted Evening from the musical South Pacific*

It Came Upon a Midnight Clear
> *—Title of a Christmas carol*

You do the hokey-pokey and turn yourself around; that's what It's all about!
> *—words from an old silly song*

Well, that's my story and I'm sticking to It.
> *—a country western song*

It Had to Be You
> *— an old song title*

How will It all work out?
I don't know. It's a mystery!
> *—from the movie Shakespeare in Love*

I don't believe any of It!
> *—an IRS auditor*

It totally changed my life.

> —*a recent lottery winner*

Don't leave home without It.

> —*an ad agency*

It really is a great deal.

> —*a used car salesman*

Round and round It goes, and where It stops (and starts) nobody knows!

> —*a carnival pitchman*

Make It so, Number One.

> —*Jean-Luc Picard, Captain, USS Enterprise*

It's a beautiful day in the neighborhood.

> —*Mr. Rogers*

Take It to the Limit

> —*a song by The Eagles*

I'm lovin' It.

> —*Ronald McDonald*

Just try It. You'll like It!

> —*your mother*

It's in the Movies!

It's a Wonderful Life

As Good as It Gets

The Girl Can't Help It

Pay It Forward

Whose Line Is It Anyway?

Say It Isn't So

It Could Happen to You

It's a Mad Mad Mad Mad World

Bring It On

It's a Beautiful Day

It's a Small World

It Came From Outer Space

It Happened One Night

It's for the Birds

It Must Be Love

It Runs in the Family

It Takes All Kinds

Blame It on Rio

Isn't It Romantic?

Are You With It?

Get Over It

As You Like It

Grin and Bear It

The Devil Made Me Do It

A River Runs Through It

Some Like It Hot

50 Possible Titles for This Book
(49 of which never got used)

1. All of It is Just for You

2. Can It Really Be True?

3. Can *This* Really Be It?

4. Enlightenment for Dummies

5. Enlightenment: is It for Real?

6. Enlightenment: What It's All About

7. Getting With the Way It Is

8. Getting With What *Is*

26. It Is What It Is

27. It's One From the Heart

28. It's One of Its Kind

29. Let It be You!

30. Look What It's Doing Now

31. Loving It the Way It Is

32. It Can Only Be You

33. So Be It

34. Take It To Heart

35. The Little Book About It

36. The Enlighten It Up Book

37. The Enlighten Up Book

38. The 30 Minute Enlightenment Book

39. The Way IT Is *(The Winner!)*

40. What Can Any of It Mean?

41. What Can It Be?

42. What Does It All Mean?

Write It Down!

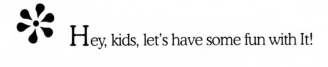 Hey, kids, let's have some fun with It!

Make your *own* list of phrases that It uses when It shows up for you. I'll even start It off:

How did It all begin?

It's for your own good.

It's in the mail.

It's demonic.

It's all screwed up!

It's later than you think.

It's a walk in the park.

It pisses me off!

It's too much!

It's a piece of cake.

It's easy as pie.

It's a slippery slope.

It tastes like chicken.

Aw, f_ _k It!

It's a bird. It's a plane. It's Superman!

Damn It anyway!

Take this job and shove It!

So, how will It all end?

_____

_____

_____

_____

_____

Letting It All
Hang Out!

❀   Well, now that you've had a chance to read (and write) about It, why don't you try sending It *a love letter from your heart?*

Just go ahead and use the next few pages to share how you're feeling about It right now.

And, if you'd rather be a bit more formal, you can even start It off like this:

To Whom It May Concern,

_____

_____

_____

_____

_____

_____

_____

_____

_____

_____

_____

_____

_____

_____

_____

_____

_____

_____

_____

About the Author

and some parting advice

Believe It or not, Chuck Hillig, MFT, worked as a state licensed psychotherapist in California for many years. He now lives in Locust Grove, Virginia. His website is chuckhillig.com.

To make It more real for you, Chuck suggests that you begin to notice just how often It seems to come up in your everyday conversations. It's true. You can't ever get away from It simply because, one way or another, you're *always* talking about It.

And (since everyone is so completely *full* of It anyway) life will become so much easier if you just open your heart and admit It all to yourself!

"It's easy to do," Chuck says, "because It's always happening in the twinkling 'I' of the beholder. So, like It or not, we're all in It together (and, of course, *vice versa*). That's what It's all about!"

Sentient Publications, LLC publishes books on cultural creativity, experimental education, transformative spirituality, holistic health, new science, ecology, and other topics, approached from an integral viewpoint. Our authors are intensely interested in exploring the nature of life from fresh perspectives, addressing life's great questions, and fostering the full expression of the human potential. Sentient Publications' books arise from the spirit of inquiry and the richness of the inherent dialogue between writer and reader.

Our Culture Tools series is designed to give social catalyzers and cultural entrepreneurs the essential information, technology, and inspiration to forge a sustainable, creative, and compassionate world.

We are very interested in hearing from our readers. To direct suggestions or comments to us, or to be added to our mailing list, please contact:

SENTIENT PUBLICATIONS, LLC
1113 Spruce Street
Boulder, CO 80302
303-443-2188
contact@sentientpublications.com
www.sentientpublications.com

More **Chuck Hillig** Books Available
from Sentient Publications

Enlightenment for Beginners
Discovering the Dance of the Divine
by Chuck Hillig
Paperback $14.95 1-59181-040-X 216 pages

Enlightenment for Beginners is the simple account of how and why you've been imagining yourself to be only a separate and limited being. Hillig invites the seeker to discover who they really are and to find that a life of love and connection is already at hand.

Looking for God
Seeing the Whole in One
by Chuck Hillig
Paperback $15.95 1-59181-059-9 110 pages

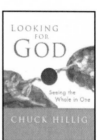

This book has a one-inch hole drilled through the center of each page, which the author uses as a metaphor for the emptiness we may fear in ourselves. By pointing to the hole, Hillig shows the spaciousness in the center of each of us and the unique journey into the (w)holeness that lies at the core of the spiritual path.

Seeds for the Soul
Living as the Source of Who You Are
by Chuck Hillig
Paperback $16.95 1-59181-062-9 270 pages

Like a good friend cutting through the confusion, Chuck Hillig takes you by the hand and leads you to where you can look reality squarely in the face. His words will quietly reverberate in the very depths of your consciousness, and whether they act as gentle reminders or loud alarm clocks, they will lovingly direct you to the only person who holds your truth: you.